Nelson Mandela

CAITLIN PROZONIC

TABLE OF CONTENTS

Early Life	2
Battling Segregation	6
Trial and Imprisonment	11
South Africa, United	14
President	17
Glossary/Index	20

PIONEER VALLEY EDUCATIONAL PRESS, INC

EARLY LIFE

When Nelson Mandela was a boy, he listened to many stories. He heard stories of how his black ancestors had shared their land and resources with white people, who took it all for themselves. And he learned about brave African kings who fought and lost wars after people from Europe invaded and took control of lands in Africa.

Nelson was inspired when he listened to these tales. Although they were not happy stories, they motivated him to want to make a difference and to help his people.

RORKE'S DRIFT

Nelson was born in South Africa in 1918 and was the son of a Thembu **chieftain**. His father taught him how to be strong in difficult situations. When Nelson's father was accused of a crime, he argued before a **magistrate**, or judge. The magistrate removed Nelson's father as chieftain, even though he had done nothing wrong. There was no trial and no evidence, but Nelson's father was still forced from his position and his home.

South Africa

Nelson and his family were forced to move to a village. It wasn't a nice place; they lived in mud huts where the floors were made from the dirt left by ant colonies. They did not have running water and had to carry water from nearby streams. And they did not own the land where they lived. This was common for black South African families; only white people could own land at that time. Nelson lived during a time when black and white people were **segregated**.

Village of Qunu, where Nelson Mandela was raised

Nelson's father died when he was still a boy, and he was welcomed back into the Thembu clan by the ruler. He was given luxuries he had not had while living in the village.

The leaders of the Thembu clan expected Nelson to take over the role of chief, but he surprised everyone by choosing another path. He wanted to fight for the rights of others, especially the black people of South Africa, so he decided to become a lawyer. It was during his law studies that he became interested in politics, a passion that would stay with him throughout his life.

Nelson Mandela's childhood home

BATTLING SEGREGATION

In 1948, a political group called the National Party came to power in South Africa. The National Party quickly made laws that separated South Africans into four categories: white, black, colored (people of mixed race), and Asian. This treatment was called **apartheid**. These laws kept people of different races separate from one another, much like the segregation laws in the United States that existed until the 1960s.

Minority white people were considered superior during apartheid, leaving black South Africans poor and without rights. Life was very difficult for black people, and they were forced to live in fenced-in, run-down villages called homelands. People were placed in the homelands based on their ethnicity, and they were permitted to leave during the day only if they had a traveling pass. At night, they had to return to their designated homeland.

More to Explore

In South Africa, many white people were worried that they would lose their jobs, culture, and language if they let all races have **EQUAL RIGHTS**.

Black people could not live in the same areas as white people or run businesses in areas that were designated for white people. They also could only use resources assigned to black people, such as entrances to public places, beaches, buses, and benches. Nonwhites had to carry passes to visit white-designated areas—even to go to their jobs. And nonwhites were not allowed to vote.

Nelson did not like these laws; he thought they were very unfair. As a lawyer, he worked on many cases to help people who suffered from the apartheid laws.

MORE TO EXPLORE

Under apartheid, **WHITE SOUTH AFRICANS** controlled more than 80 percent of the nation's land, even though they made up less than 20 percent of the population.

He also joined a group called the African National Congress (ANC), which organized nonviolent protests against racial **discrimination**. Nelson traveled around South Africa campaigning for black South Africans' rights, such as the right to vote and the right to protest apartheid laws.

But the government did not agree with Nelson's ideas, and he was arrested multiple times.

MORE TO EXPLORE

In 1960, the **SOUTH AFRICAN GOVERNMENT** banned the ANC, so the ANC began to operate underground, hiding their work from the government to avoid getting caught.

TRIAL AND IMPRISONMENT

In 1964, Nelson was accused of working against the government. During the trial, Nelson gave a four-hour speech. He admitted to some of the charges against him, even though he faced the death penalty. Seven weeks later, he and seven other men were convicted and sentenced to life in prison.

Nelson Mandela

" I have cherished the ideal of a democratic and free society in which all persons live together in harmony and with equal opportunities. It is an ideal which I hope to live for and to achieve. "

— NELSON MANDELA

Nelson was in prison for many years. He and the other inmates had to do hard labor, like making gravel out of large stones. The conditions were not very good, and he and other prisoners suffered.

Nelson's mother and his oldest son died while he was in prison, but he was not allowed to go to their funerals. He also contracted **tuberculosis**, a dangerous infection of the lungs.

MORE TO EXPLORE

The South African government tried twice to make deals with Nelson to set him free, but Nelson always rejected them. He said that only **FREE MEN** could make such deals, and he was not a free man.

But even from inside his prison cell, Nelson still found a way to make a difference. He encouraged his fellow prisoners to use nonviolent protests against apartheid and the government.

Outside the prison, black South Africans used Nelson as a symbol against apartheid. They continued to fight segregation in his name.

SOUTH AFRICA, UNITED

In the mid- to late 1980s, government officials met with Nelson to talk to him about the possibility of making changes to the terrible laws that separated people.

MORE TO EXPLORE

Many people expressed their **DISAPPROVAL OF APARTHEID** and constantly encouraged South Africans, as well as people all over the world, to fight it.

On February 11, 1990, after 27 years in prison, Nelson Mandela was released. He was once again united with his family and his people to be a champion for civil rights in South Africa.

Before long, Nelson became the leader of the ANC, and he worked closely with the new president of South Africa to end apartheid. Together, they created a new constitution for South Africa to eliminate segregation and the unfair laws that had been in force for so many years. This new constitution took effect in 1994, officially ending apartheid. Now all people in South Africa could interact with one another, no matter the color of their skin.

MORE TO EXPLORE

Nelson Mandela and President F. W. de Klerk jointly won the **NOBEL PEACE PRIZE** in 1993 for their work to end apartheid.

PRESIDENT

With the end of apartheid, a new era began in South Africa. People of all races could vote, and in 1994, they elected Nelson Mandela as the new president of South Africa. He was the nation's first black president.

While in office, Nelson focused on helping people, just as he had dreamed of doing when he was a child. He improved the housing, education, and economic situations of black South Africans and instituted a new democratic constitution that would help make all South Africans equal.

In December 2013, Nelson Mandela died at the age of 95. He lived his life fighting for freedom, equality, and education for all people. He believed that if "people are determined, they can do anything."

MORE TO EXPLORE

In 2009, the Nelson Mandela Foundation founded **MANDELA DAY** to be celebrated on July 18 to honor his dedication to making the world a better place and to inspire others to do the same.

Nelson Mandela Timeline

1918	Nelson Mandela was born
1944	Joined the African National Congress
1948	Apartheid became official in South Africa
1964	Sentenced to life in prison
1990	Released from prison
1993	Won the Nobel Peace Prize
1994	Elected as the first black president of South Africa
2009	The first observance of Mandela Day
2013	Nelson Mandela died

Bantustans

Bantustans, or homelands, were the territories in South Africa where black South Africans were forced to live. Here is a map of the different Bantustans in South Africa during apartheid.

Bantustan Territories

- Bophuthatswana
- Ciskei
- Gazankulu
- KaNgwane
- KwaNdebele
- KwaZulu
- Lebowa
- QwaQwa
- Transkei
- Venda
- - - Historical province boundaries

GLOSSARY

apartheid
racial segregation in South Africa

chieftain
the leader of a clan or tribe

discrimination
hatred toward a person or group of people because of prejudice

magistrate
a local government official who can also act as a judge

minority
a group that is a smaller part of a larger group

segregated
separated from people who are of a different race or ethnicity

tuberculosis
a disease of the lungs that is very contagious and can be deadly

INDEX

African National Congress (ANC) 10, 16, 19
apartheid 6–7, 9–10, 13, 14, 16, 17, 19
arrested 10, 11
chieftain 3
constitution 16, 17
convicted 11
discrimination 10
father 3, 5
government 10, 11, 12, 13, 14, 20
homelands 7
laws 6, 9, 10, 14, 16
lawyer 5, 9
magistrate 3
Mandela Day 18, 19
minority 7
National Party 6
Nelson Mandela Foundation 18
Nobel Peace Prize 16, 19
president 16, 17, 19
prison 11–13, 15, 19
Qunu 4
rights 5, 7, 10, 15
segregated 4
segregation 6, 13, 16, 20
South Africa 3, 5, 6, 7, 10, 15, 16, 17, 19, 20
Thembu 3, 5
trial 3, 11
tuberculosis 12
village 4, 5, 7
vote 8, 10, 17